To: Daniel & Amber . . .
On a cold winter's night,
when you have nothing else to do,
pick up this book,
and read a poem, or two.

SHOWERING WITH LIZARDS
(POEMS AND PROSE OF THE DESERT SOUTHWEST)

MARY RUTH WEAVER

authorHOUSE

AuthorHouse™
1663 Liberty Drive
Bloomington, IN 47403
www.authorhouse.com
Phone: 833-262-8899

© 2020 Mary Ruth Weaver. All rights reserved.

No part of this book may be reproduced, stored in a retrieval system, or transmitted by any means without the written permission of the author.

Published by AuthorHouse 10/31/2020

ISBN: 978-1-6655-0361-7 (sc)
ISBN: 978-1-6655-0373-0 (e)

Print information available on the last page.

Any people depicted in stock imagery provided by Getty Images are models, and such images are being used for illustrative purposes only.
Certain stock imagery © Getty Images.

This book is printed on acid-free paper.

Because of the dynamic nature of the Internet, any web addresses or links contained in this book may have changed since publication and may no longer be valid. The views expressed in this work are solely those of the author and do not necessarily reflect the views of the publisher, and the publisher hereby disclaims any responsibility for them.

DEDICATION

To all the poets,
dreamers, naturalists, and desert rats who enjoy the great outdoors, and all the many treasures it holds.

ACKNOWLEDGEMENT

I have enjoyed writing stories and poetry all my life. Living in the desert has given me many opportunities to write and explore the desert southwest.

Many things in Yuma and around Arizona gave me ideas and inspirations to write the many poems in this book. My Creative Writing Professor, David Coy, assigned the class a writing project one day: write a poem about a picture in the newspaper, or magazine. I saw a picture on the front page of our local newspaper of a friend, Bill Jewett, getting ready to launch his hot air balloon. He was my inspiration for a poem on page 69, so thank you Bill for the inspiration.

One day I met a nurse. She introduced herself as Misty. I told her that was a beautiful name, and I would have to write a poem about her name to add to my collection. I wrote a poem about a misty morning in Yuma. That poem can be found on page 39 of this book. Many thanks to Misty for her kindness and professionalism, and her inspiration for one of my poems.

My sister, Barbara, suggested I write a poem about one of our favorite restaurants in Yuma; Chile Pepper. So, I wrote one, and with The Gutierrez Family's permission, it is published on page 11.

My heartfelt thanks to my husband, Gary, my daughter, Vikki, and my son, John who give me continual support on my writing.

And, my life wouldn't be complete without my three beautiful grandchildren, Gracie, Mattie, and Finn. They inspire me to continue writing and publishing my books to leave them a legacy.

AMERICA'S VALENTINE

Ghosts towns, copper mines, and gold.
Mysterious treasure hidden in Superstitious Mountain
for treasure hunters to find, young and old.

Kachina dolls, Kokopelli dancers, and Yei.
Superstitious trinkets coveted by the natives
for ceremonies to chant over and pray.

Hot air balloon launches into space,
makes the skies dance with excitement
as they put on a new face.

Fifteen hundred miles of river flowing to the south,
heading for the Gulf of California,
ending up at its mouth.

The magnificent sunsets that bid goodnight to the day,
are surpassed only by the beautiful mornings
that are soon on their way.

Arizona State, the 48th of its kind,
admitted to the Union on February 14, 1912,
a Valentine of sorts, a very rare find.

BIGHORN PROUD

How robust, sturdy, and stout he appears
climbing up mountainous terrain
with the surety and confidence
afforded him by his large size
and beautifully curved horns.

Master of his class he climbs and stops and looks about
surveying the mountainside for
food, predators, or ewes
who may be prime to mate with and
bring forth an acceptable offspring.

Bighorn Sheep *(Ovis canadensis nelsoni)*
roams the mountainsides of southern Arizona
proud, protective, and regal
dominating the rocky surroundings
and making sure all is well and guarded.

I observed his majestic physique
that brisk fall day in Palm Canyon
as he paraded about and proclaimed his space
as I cautiously watched from afar
quietly focusing my binoculars so as not to disturb.

With all the courage of a warrior
this ram stands erect, proud, and convinced
that his strength and gallantry
will establish a dominance hierarchy
to secure a place for him and his pride.

BLACK WIDOW TERROR

Black as night
lurking in the corner.
Your red hourglass symbol
warns me to be cautious.

I move slowly
watching to see if you will run and hide.
The thought of your bite
frightens me so.

Holding my breath
I take aim, position my body,
and zoom in steady and direct,
and zot! The bug spray relieves my terror.

BORDER STATE

"Chicklet, chicklet, chicklet," they cry,
as I cross over the border into Mexico.
Those small little, sun-tanned children,
seeking a few pennies, by selling gum to the Americans.

The streets are lined with vendors,
selling beautifully colored blankets,
and coyotes and donkeys fashioned into ceramics,
to adorn our lawns.

No chance to get hungry here,
for taco and burrito stands are abundant,
and soft drinks, unlike our brands,
quench the thirst and satisfy the palate.

Less than ten miles from home,
I can visit a foreign country,
have a taco on the streets,
or enjoy a fine meal in a local restaurant.

Portions are overwhelming,
for these are a generous people,
courteous, kind, and eager to please
the tourists who flock here daily.

Algodones, Mexico,
one of the cities bordering the U. S.,
offering sights and smells,
tastes and variety, so different from our own.

CACTUS

Cinquain

Cactus
Prickly Pear
Red, juicy fruit
Nectar of the desert
Satiating

CACTUS GARDEN

Haiku

Cactus all around
Miles of Saguaro, Prickly Pear
Nature's garden

CACTUS WREN

Rising early one spring morning,
I heard the chattering of a Cactus Wren
as she fussed and primped and made a nest
in my backyard high atop a Saguaro Cactus.

Fussing and fretting, she made sure
the nest was well prepared for her
clutch of eggs that she would lay and
then anxiously wait for their arrival.

Not one to be left pacing and waiting
her mate is kept busy during this time
as he not only cares for the young once hatched,
but also prepares a second or third nest for her next brood.

This skittish little bird would often scream
or bark at our dogs if they got too near the cactus
while she was building and preparing the nest,
and her noisy scolding quickly drove them away.

How beautiful are their creamy colored brown feathers
and the white stripe extending just behind the eye
all the way down to the middle of the back
with the beak appearing slightly curved.

(Campylorhynchus brunneicapillus), is translated as
curved beak for the Cactus Wren,
a beautiful creature that can live up to ten years
and is the state bird of Arizona.

CHILE PEPPER

Chile pepper, chile pepper,
delicious, spicy, hot.
Put 'em on my tacos,
cook 'em in a pot.

One pepper, two peppers,
three peppers, four,
get out the water,
and quickly bolt the door.

Eating chile peppers,
makes my eyes sting,
but I just wouldn't trade them,
for any other thing.

Carne Asada,
I couldn't eat without,
those chile, chile peppers,
that's what it's all about.

So revered in Yuma,
and the pepper's claim to fame,
a very favorite restaurant,
Chile Pepper® is its name.*

*Permission from The Gutierrez Family, owners of Chile Pepper Restaurant, to use their name.

COME, SWEET BIRDS

Come, sweet birds, to the garden,
And the tree I have watered and grown,
To provide for you safe shelter,
And a home you can call your own.

Come, sweet birds, to the garden,
And the food I have scattered and hung,
To provide for you sweet substance,
And a meal for a song to be sung.

Come, sweet birds, to the garden,
And the water I have filled in the bowl,
To provide for you cool moisture,
And a drink to nourish your soul.

Come, sweet birds, to the garden,
And to the care I have learned to love,
To provide for you and all creatures,
As a command from God up above.

CRICKET, CRICKET, CRICKET

Cricket, cricket, cricket,
I looked high and low, in every room,
in every corner of the house
for the chirping of the
cricket, cricket, cricket.

Cricket, cricket, cricket,
where are you hiding
making that annoying
chirping sound of a
cricket, cricket, cricket.

Cricket, cricket, cricket,
how many are there
cranking out that irritating sound
of a little, bitty
cricket, cricket, cricket.

Cricket, cricket, cricket,
must you taunt me
in the middle of the night with
that aggravating, bothersome sound of a
cricket, cricket, cricket.

Cricket, cricket, cricket,
I count the chirps as you rub your legs together
turning out that annoyING,
irriTATING, aggRAVATING,
boTHERSOME, MADDENING sound of a
CRICKET!

DELIGHTFUL TREAT

What a delightful treat I came upon,
that late April evening my first year in Arizona.

This tall, enormous cactus full of needles
was blooming delicate, white flowers.

I was amazed at its beauty, and snapped a photo
hoping to find more information about this amazing plant.

Since this cactus was on my community college campus,
I showed the picture to my professor.

Carnegiea gigantea, he said, the Saguaro cactus.
It's beautiful flower is the state wildflower.

Their flowers appear in April through June,
and open well after sunset and close in mid-afternoon.

As the bloom dies, it forms a delicious ruby red fruit,
that Tohono O'odham tribes have utilized for years.

They harvest the fruit as a drink for celebrating
the beginning of summer planting season.

O'odhams believe that the bright red fruit
will summon the rains to nourish their crops.

How could such an unassuming plant
be so useful in providing food, drink, and tools.

Shelter is derived from the Saguaro's ribs,
while spines become sewing needles and
a dead cactus a boot for storage.

That year was exciting to learn about plants,
and the phenomenal state protected Saguaro.

DESERT LIFE

Dust storms, with blowing sand,
harsh, hot living
in a dry, parched land.

Cactus with needles,
point of pain,
growing wild with or without rain.

Scurrying lizards,
out in the sun,
snatching up bugs one by one.

Tree frogs croaking,
in the midnight air,
happily singing without a care.

Occasional rainfall,
is quite a relief,
more of the same is beyond belief.

DESERT MARINES

The few, the proud, the Marines,
as their motto firmly agrees,
they protect, and serve, and defend,
on the land, in the air, and the seas.

They train in this remote, arid desert,
to be ready to fight over there,
against those who threaten our homeland,
no enemy would ever dare.

I watch as they fly overhead,
as they swoop, and dip, and climb,
for these brave pilots who dedicate their lives,
flight training is a crucial time.

For love of the land, they pledge their heart,
for love of the sea they vow to preserve,
for love of the air they soar on high,
patrolling the skies of the country they serve.

When it comes time to test their training,
I pray that God will honor their call,
and keep them safe for the sake of their families,
and the fate of their enemies to fall.

DESERT SNOW

Giant Saguaro, what are you doing,
standing there with snow on your head and arms?
You live in the Sonoran Desert,
and should be sweating and dusty from heat and sand.

You stand there regal and tall,
in Tucson, Arizona where you live,
soaking in the soft, wet snow
that you very seldom see, but welcome.

Tucson—too-sawn, the Spanish so-named,
but the name is derived from the
O'odham Indian word *Cuk **S**on*,
meaning "at the base of the black hill."

The black hill we speak of,
is the hill formed by volcanic ash
billions of years ago.

DESERT SUN

Haiku

Hot, hot desert sun
Burning down upon the sand
Waiting for the night

DUCKS AT THE EDGE OF THE RIVER

The ducks at the edge of the river,
they quack, and waddle, and wade,
so glad to be in the water,
they cool off as they happily bathe.

The ducks at the edge of the river,
just grateful to be out of the heat,
cool water refreshes their feathers,
bathing cools down their tired, hot feet.

The ducks at the edge of the river,
come out and step onto the land,
they fluff and primp and fritter,
while standing on the dry, hot sand.

The ducks at the edge of the river,
are a pleasure to watch and feed,
they snatch up the free corn morsels,
shelter, water, food, and rest is all they need.

DUST DEVIL

Dust Devil
twirling fast across the land.
You formed a funnel
out of sand, debris, and the hot desert wind.

You form in no particular season,
for I've seen you in cold March winds,
and hot, summer monsoons.
Your tornado-like shape looks ominous, but harmless.

The Navajo call you *chiindii*, (*ch'įįdii*)
for they believe you are the ghost left behind
when a Navajo dies,
and watch to see which way you spin.

Clockwise means you are a good spirit,
and counter-clockwise, a bad spirit,
and the chiindii must not be touched,
for the bad chiindii may cause illness or death.

I respect the Navajo religion and their beliefs,
but the dust devils to me are fun to watch,
but something to avoid, for the sand and debris,
can irritate the skin, and injure the eyes.

EARLY MORNING QUIET

The early morning quiet woke me.
No A/C running,
and the window I left open last night
was delivering a soft, cool breeze.

Early mornings in Yuma.
Quiet, peaceful, relaxing,
to the point I sometimes go back to sleep,
and miss that early morning task I had planned.

When I don't fall back to sleep,
I prepare a plate of eggs, bacon, and toast,
pull up a chair at the patio table,
and sip hot coffee as I listen to the birds.

Although they break the early morning quiet,
their singing adds to the silence.
With a comforting breakfast in front of me,
the quiet, plus the singing, rejuvenates my soul.

I know I have many things to do today,
but the peace I get now
will carry me through the day,
because of this early morning quiet.

EARLY MORNING RAIN

I awoke with the sound of rain
softly patting the rooftop, window, and ground.

Not wanting to get out of bed,
because the soothing sound was so comforting,
I lay there for a moment and sighed.

But because rain is so rare in this desert town,
I wanted to enjoy its very short visit.

So, I got up and opened the patio door,
and breathed in the cool, refreshing moisture
as the rain fell softly, and the wind blew gently.

The flowers, trees, and grass
drank in its delicious, sweet nectar.

Oh, the sweet smell of the sudden shower
from above gave me pause to reflect on
the many blessings I have received.

It was a time to forget problems and difficulties of life,
because I could save those for another day.

Now, at this moment, the world was renewed
as I closed my eyes and took in a deep breath,
reassured that all was right with the world.

FLOW RIVER FLOW

It charges south like a wild horse unbridled and free,
Stampeding up against the banks
And slamming its strength into the
open spaces left by time.

With speed and agility unmatched by its peers,
It rears its head upwards
And rushes uncontrollably to freedom.

Demanding its right to inhabit the wide-open spaces,
It thrusts forward on its journey of life
Wasting no time dominating its place on earth.

With all its raging power and strength,
How gentle it can turn as it nears an open space
That waits to embrace its mighty impact.

Its majestic and powerful body is magnificent,
As it abruptly turns west
And winds its way through the great Grand Canyon.

Not stopping there,
It quickly turns southward
And meanders gracefully towards a series of dams.

Racing with the wind,
It briefly pauses
To take a sip from the Hardy River.

As it snorts and breathes freely,
It gets a second wind
Refusing to be harnessed and confined.

And after traveling nearly fifteen hundred miles,
Reaches its final destination,
In the Gulf of California.

Revered, protected, and prized,
No one can completely tame,
The grand Colorado River.

GEM OF THE SOUTHWEST

Cinquain

Turquoise
Precious stone
Copper mining discovery
State gem of Arizona
Lovely

GOPHER

Cinquain

Gopher
Underground rodent
Tears up gardens
Looks so very cute
Destructive

HUMMINGBIRD

Cinquain

Hummingbird
flying fast
sweet and lovely
hovering over the flowers
Humming

HUMMINGBIRD FLITTING

Haiku

Hummingbird, so small
Flits from flower to flower
Territorial

HUMMINGBIRD NESTING

Hummingbird nesting
so small and so sweet
how gently you fluff and primp
as you prepare your nest.

I observed you in my Italian Cypress tree
as you made sure you were high enough
and safe enough from prying eyes
and lurking predators.

Your tiny three inch body and less
than an ounce body weight
make you one of the tiniest birds in my garden
and your beautiful iridescent feathers
are a delight to watch as you flit about.

You feast on the Cape Cod Honeysuckle
I planted alongside the brick wall
and devour its sweet succulent nectar
to replenish nourishment lost while flying.

The red Verbena growing up against the wooden fence
provides an alternative flavor for your daily meal
that must be replaced many times throughout the day
and provide half your weight in daily food.

You hover gently over an Indian Paintbrush plant
with its vermillion-red flowers
and then fly backwards, forwards, up and down
defying all manner of modern-day aircraft.

How adorable you were
the morning I saw you sitting on my clothesline
thinking I had left a wooden clothespin
but you quickly lifted off and made me smile.

You belong to the *Trochilidae* family
and your feet are only used for perching
as you did that morning on my clothesline
causing me to delight in your talent and beauty.

Stay with me little flying jewels
so that I may feed and nurture you
and sustain you throughout the year
and for many more to come.

KOKOPELLI DANCERS

Haiku

Kokopelli Dancers
Dancing under the stars
Chanting out prayers

LONGING FOR RAIN

Parched, dry, brittle shards of green paint
flaked off the sides of the old, worn and tattered tool shed
as two gray Mourning doves hovered clumsily overhead
then alit on its hot, searing rooftop.

Touching briefly, they quickly lifted off
and sought relief on a nearby waiting mesquite branch
where hot, scratchy leaves brushed
warmly against their wings,
and warned of an evening of muggy, restless sleep.

Summer advanced quickly into the hot
and humid monsoon season,
with its taunting one-hundred degree plus temperatures,
and blinding, almost unbearable, desert sun
that scorched wilting plants into an
unrecognizable mass of fodder.

Watching there, I ran my fingers
down the side of a fence post,
tracing a crack that the harsh,
blistering weather had created,
and with an almost trance-fixed motion,
pulled at it until it almost formed a
perfectly shaped post again.

With hot, sticky perspiration running
down the sides of my face,
I removed my straw hat and work gloves,
and roughly wiped the sweat off with
the edge of my shirt sleeve,
as the burning wind kicked up a dust devil
that danced along the edge of the fence.

Hearing the rustle of dry brush moved by the wind,
I turned to catch a glimpse of a lizard
dart out from the side of a rock,
and with stealth-like precision and accuracy,
snatched up a bug with its tongue.

The heat was well upon us in this quiet desert town,
as I longed for the mild, spring-like winters
that drew thousands of visitors
to our small community each year.

Smelling charcoal lighter fluid from a backyard barbecue,
my stomach churned as the thought
of food being prepared
on this sizzling hot day
made me nauseous and weak.

Gathering up my tools, I caught
the scent of rain in the air,
as I headed for the house,
in search of a cold glass of water
to replenish the fluids lost while working.

Tasting the water as if for the first time,
I leaned back in my chair, closed my eyes,
and sighed as the far off sound of thunder,
made me long for the rain that was to come.

MARSH FEEDING WONDER

Sweet, little White-faced Ibis,
your long de-curved bill makes it easy
to scoop up morsels of food
as you wade across the wetlands
enjoying the warmer climate and gentle winds
of southwestern winter months.

Your long-legged stance is an asset to you
as you glide across the marshes,
all of two feet tall, and display your
iridescent bronze, purple, and green plumage,
with your white-bordered reddish face
and occasionally flaunt your three-foot wingspan.

Threskiornithidae, your semi-nomadic lifestyle
allows me to observe you one year, and
then the next I long for your return
to the West Wetlands of Yuma, Arizona
where local conservationists labor annually
to ensure your safe return and re-population.

Our dry, almost rain-free climate
keeps you longing for those rare, sudden rainfalls
that fill the wetlands with much needed moisture

and temporary flooding
to create a secure breeding habitat
and assure your species does not become extinct.

Wade and feed and grow with purpose
to recreate your beautiful presence
in an environment that allows you the freedom
to enjoy these dense lowlands
along the southwestern border of Mexico,
and emerge as an added beauty to
these natural surroundings.

MISTY MORNING

Yuma has beautiful weather,
at least nine months out of the year.
When it rains, we love it,
when the wind blows harshly, we endure it.

When the hot summer months,
bring the monsoon season,
we batten down the hatches,
and ride out the storm.

But when nature throws us a curve,
and changes all the rules,
we wonder if we are still in the desert,
or dislocated to San Francisco!

So, you can imagine my surprise,
that early morning in October,
when I headed out for work,
and the air was blanketed with a layer of fog!

Fog, in Yuma, with all its heat, sand, and desert?
Where did this come from?
Although uncommon, especially in Yuma,
sudden fog is rare and disturbing.

Disturbing, because we don't know what to do with it.
Rare, because we're in the desert.
Uncommon, because ninety percent of our days are sunny.
So, how do we handle a foggy day?

For me, I drove to work slowly.
When I got to work, joined in the talk about the fog,
and enjoyed the misty morning,
as the fog began to lift and dissipate.

A misty morning in Yuma,
rare, uncommon, disturbing,
but a change from the heat, the sun,
and the occasional rain.

MONSOON MADNESS

Hot, sticky, humid, uncomfortable,
the weatherman reports.
No rain in sight.
Only more of the same.
When will the rains come
to wash away this stickiness?
When will the cool winds blow
to end this mugginess?
When will this temperature change
to cool down the air?
When, when, when will the madness end?
The Monsoon madness that tethers the skin.
The madness of the Monsoon
that rips at the soul.
The madness, madness, madness
we call Sheol.

MONSTER IN THE DESERT

Gila Monster, great warrior of the desert.
Your colorful, beaded skin camouflages your presence.
We watch from afar,
because your venomous bite may not kill,
but make us violently ill.

So sluggish, you pose little threat to humans,
for we believe we can outrun you,
and avoid any direct contact,
because you mostly hide in burrows, and under rocks,
but still, we keep our distance.

If we see you, we assume you are only looking for food,
those small animals, birds, insects, lizards, and frogs.
Although you look like you could swallow us whole,
you mainly eat bird and reptile eggs,
and eat only five to ten times a year.

Heloderma suspectum, meaning studded skin,
and Gila from the Gila River
in which you have spent most of your time in the past.
Now you settle for succulent desert, and burrows
near water or moisture, on which you thrive.

I snapped a picture of you that rainy, summer day,
after a sudden, refreshing rainfall.
You immersed yourself in the small puddle of rainwater,
and enjoyed flopping around
soaking in the water and happy to be alive.

NIGHT SOLDIER

Cinquain

Scorpion
Venomous arachnid
Emerging at night
Glows under black light
Lethal

NOCTURNAL FEAST

She slithers out cautiously
from beneath the cool sand
looking for rodents, lizards, and toads
to satisfy her midnight hunger
as her young wait for her return.

Too hot to hunt during the day
she sleeps under the hot sand
with horned scales protecting her eyes
waiting for nighttime
to feast on the surrounding cuisine.

Crotalus cerastes, the Sidewinder Rattlesnake
pale, brown, with dark patches
will make its move as soon as it
notices a scrumptious delight
wandering away from its safe abode.

Fast, coordinated, and intent
Mrs. Sidewinder makes her move
in sidewinding fashion
leaving a "J-shaped" pattern on the sand
behind her as she travels to scoop up her prey.

A large lizard looks good
as she administers a small bite of venom
just around the throat
holding it in her mouth until the kill
becomes limp and gives up the fight.

She would have preferred a rodent
but biting it and then letting it go
to follow until it became too incapacitated to walk
would have been too much trouble for her
on this hot, humid evening.

Satisfied with her repast
she returns to her burrow to care for her young
she has birthed in the early morning hours
to protect them a few days until they set out
to explore life on their own.

NOVEMBER CLOUDS

They form when no one's looking,
they show up when no one's around,
they shape into shapes that are funny,
a rabbit, a dragon, a clown.

They're fun to look at and study,
they're fun to imagine and dream,
they're fun to watch when they change quickly,
an elephant, a dog, whipped cream.

Sometimes they can appear threatening,
sometimes a hope for rain,
sometimes a covering for comfort,
a softness, a roughness, or plain.

No matter how they look,
no matter which form you can guess,
no matter the animal they mimic,
November clouds are sure to impress.

PARCHED

Cinquain

Parched
Scratchy throat
Dry, cracked lips
High noon desert sun
Thirst

PEACEFUL PALO VERDE

So delicate, beautiful, and peaceful.
You stand erect, immobile,
with light green bark that looks like you are a young plant,
but I know you have been growing for many years.

Those soft, yellow flowers blooming in April and May,
makes my heart leap at its beauty.
Although you provide a respite for
me, you also provide shade
in the summer for Saguaro cactus, and
warmth for them in winter.

Parkinsonia aculeata, your genus name,
and Palo Verde is Spanish for green stick.
Your canopy makes you a nurse for the cactus,
as you lovingly care for its health.

Sometimes we think only humans can have these qualities,
but you bring a humanness to your species.
What must you be thinking as you stand there,
so caring, loving, and peaceful.

PEOPLE OF THE DESERT

Walk tall
People of the desert
assert your pride in the land that you love.

You endured
the scorching hot days
and the long chilly nights.

Your people
tamed the wild terrain
with patience and love.

The Prickly Pear Cactus
soon became a succulent salad
when needles were removed.

And its little red fruit
a savory jelly
spread atop fresh fry bread.

You built pueblo houses
with the rich sand, adobe, and clay
of the land.

And drew water from the river
with beautifully decorated pottery
you crafted and shaped.

For the girls
you took wet clay
And shaped it into a doll.

And the boys
you cut a young branch
and formed a bow.

Your women
gathered at the water's edge
to beat the clothing against the rocks.

To remove
the dust and soil
of many days.

Your men
met to discuss
the next hunt, and rules to follow.

And made a pact
to protect and keep
your people safe.

Pipes were smoked
in total agreement
and surety that all would be obeyed.

How faithful
you have been to the land, the trees,
the plants, and animals of the earth.

To insure
they will be here
for years to come.

You have been kind
to Mother Earth
and She has been good to you.

PRAYING MANTIS PREYING

How strange and interesting
the Praying Mantis
hands poised in praying stance.

How beautiful and serene
with pious regality
looking about hands folded motionless.

The *Anthropoda Insecta Mantodea*
seems innocently harmless
in silence waiting to pounce.

So righteous and timid
it sits erect
hoping to satisfy voracious hunger.

I respect its space
watching it prepare
to eat aphids and mosquitoes.

To nibble on spiders
beetles, moths, leafhoppers
that lazily saunter about unaware.

How strange and interesting
this Praying Mantis
preying on happy little bugs.

PRISON HILL

On Prison Hill,
here sits,
the Yuma Territorial Prison.

Built in 1875,
It housed seven prisoners,
in July, 1876.

The Depression came,
in the 1920s,
and it housed hobos and the homeless.

After the prison closed, in 1910,
Yuma Union High School
occupied it as a school until 1914.

After their unexpected football win,
the Phoenix team called them "criminals",
which they proudly adopted as their nickname.

A state park and museum,
on Prison Hill resides a prison of which
a movie has been made.

3:10 To Yuma, a 1957 movie,
about a prisoner being transferred
from Contention City, Arizona to Yuma.

A riveting must-see movie,
Yuma finally gets its prisoner
when he is brought to Prison Hill.

QUECHAN PEOPLE

They are a beautiful tribe of people,
so kind, so friendly, so proud.
Living just north of the Mexican border
along the Colorado River
in southern California and Arizona.

Quechan they are called today,
and in the past The Yuma Indians.
Pronounced *kwit-saan,* meaning
'those who descended'
believing they came down to earth
from a sacred mountain.

How spiritual, I thought
when I learned what their name meant,
to hear of a people whose history and beliefs
makes reference to another place, another time,
and another way of living.

Avikwame,
the sacred mountain of which they speak,
and their legendary mythological hero, Kukumat,
whose son, Kumastamxo, gave them bows and arrows,
and showed them how to cure illnesses,

before they descended and settled
south of the Mojave Desert.

They live and laugh and love.
They believe in spiritual dreams,
healings, honoring their dead,
and protecting their land,
to preserve for generation to come.

RABBIT HIDING

Cinquain

Rabbit
Fluffy white
Hiding in garden
Munching newly grown lettuce
Harmless

RIVER RAFTING

Haiku

Slow, river rafting
Down Colorado River
Quiet, peaceful float

ROADRUNNER SHY

I watched him, quietly,
peeking from my bedroom window
as he skittered and bent,
and cocked his head from side to side.

As fast as he could,
he ran to the slice of bacon
I had secretly placed on the patio bench,
to entice my little friend to eat.

Snatching up the bacon
with his long, sharp beak,
he checked again with head cocked back and forth,
to ensure no danger lurked nearby.

He nibbled and chewed,
then swallowed whole
the bacon delight I had offered in jest,
to persuade my shy friend to perform.

SHOWERING WITH LIZARDS

With mud-crusted shoes, and hands dirtied
with the soft, moist October earth,
I stepped into a warm shower to hose off a
morning's worth of gardening and weeding.

Lingering under the cascading water,
I sighed as the water dropped rhythmically over my
body, then trickled down my back and tickled by toes.

Thinking of the tomatoes, zucchini,
bell peppers and green beans,
I salivated at the thought of fried green tomatoes
and the first fresh taste of zucchini casserole.

Transplanted from my Tennessee roots,
I have learned to reverse the seasons in this hot,
dry desert climate, in order to grow the same types
of fruits and vegetables enjoyed as a child.

Tomatoes are harvested and done by June,
while my sister in Iowa will wait until July to
begin picking and adding hers to a salad.

As she prepares for an Octoberfest, I dig, weed,
and plant my crop, then wait for Mother Earth
to present me with the fruits of my labor.

Arizona heat can be fierce and unforgiving during the summer months, but the mild winter season makes you forget the scorching, and sometimes humid-drenched days.

I resumed the feel of the water cleansing my body, as I again felt the water tickling my toes, and then something brush across my wet foot.

Looking down, I jerked back as I caught sight of a lizard that had wandered in beneath the small crack in the door, to join in my bathing ritual.

Laughing, I realized my friend was just thirsty, but harmless as he scurried up the shower wall, then back down and out the door, as another lizard, taking his lead, exited with him.

Knowing they would be lurking around later as I watered my newly-planted garden, I had to smile at the thought of explaining to my friends later how I had spent the morning showering with lizards.

SING, SING, SING

The hot, muggy summer rain had ended.
I pushed open the patio door,
smelled the fresh, clean air,
then lay on the floor to enjoy the quiet, calm night.

Immediately I heard the gentle croaking of the toads.
They sang out, as they always do,
after a heavy rain.
That weak, low-pitched whistling screech.

Many think it is annoying,
but I find it peaceful and relaxing.
They sing, out to attract a mate,
lay eggs and spawn those cute, squiggly tadpoles.

My kids scooped them up one day,
and brought them home in a bucket.
Cute little tadpoles, but we quickly returned them
to their rightful home to feed and
metamorphosis into toads.

Incilius alvarius - Sonoran Desert Toad, they are called.
They will quickly change into toads,
seek out food and shelter,
grow into adult toads, and search out a mate,
as they sing, sing, sing.

SUDDEN RAIN

The rain had stopped suddenly that April morning,
before I had a chance to see it coming down.

I got to see the dark, cloudy sky, and the few drops of rain
on my grapefruit tree, as I picked a
fresh grapefruit for breakfast.

The temperature had been 95º the day before,
and today it had dropped to a cool 63.

Since it was a much cooler day, I
decided to pick a few weeds,
and spruce up my garden after breakfast.

I began weeding, and hoeing, and
smoothing out the ground,
when a light sprinkling of rain began
gently coating my hair.

Oh, how refreshing it felt as I continued working,
and then remembering the time I
was in Ketchikan, Alaska.

As I stepped off the bus, the tour
guide offered me an umbrella,
which I politely refused, because I
wanted to feel the misting rain.

Their annual rainfall is 280 inches,
and in Yuma it comes down less than three inches a year.

I continued working the garden in the rain,
until the sprinkling became a downpour.

I gathered up my tools,
and took shelter on the patio, enjoying
the fresh smell of rain.

Although I had missed the first rain,
this sudden rain was unexpected, but much appreciated.

SUNSET

Cinquain

Sunset
Glowing orange
Gently going down
End of summer's day
Rest

SWEET DOVE

Sweet dove,
I found you one morning
when my dog tried to catch you,
and bruised your wing.

So fragile,
I comforted you quickly,
and placed you on the patio
under a laundry basket with holes.

Each day I nurtured you,
gave you water and seeds,
and let you out each time
to see if you were well enough to fly.

So sweet and trusting,
little *Inca Dove*,
you grew stronger each day,
and healed within a week.

That last day, after feeding,
I lifted the basket,
and you flew away,
with dignity and grace.

Fly little dove, fly,
and return again soon,
where food and water will be yours,
and a promise of a safe place to nest.

THE BALLOONIST
(Dedicated to Bill Jewett, Yuma, Arizona)

with early
morning anticipation he
hauls the limp lifeless hot air
balloon to the silent waiting launching
field and prepares it for an escape into the
hollow chambers of space then gently caresses
its silk billowy folds that blossom and bulge into
a giant breathing heaving mass he alone controls
with pride and patience of a well-seasoned traveler
he pulls and tugs and jostles the lines to help direct
its course although the mighty obstinate balloon
will attempt to take its commands from the wind
at its release he marvels at the ease in which
he manipulates the hulk of power above his
head to fill the skies with the graceful
magic of cloth dancing in the wind
unbridled he gently floats above
the hurried chaotic world
contented to be alone
as his body and
soul humbly
agree
his

spirit has
be come
a part of
the wind

THE TUMBLEWEED DANCE

As cool winds blow
across dry, scratchy sand

Dry, leafless tumbleweeds
dance across the fields

Mimicking ballerinas
eager to please the crowd.

With rolling, hopping, and skipping,
the frolicking tumbleweeds

Dance the dance
with windblown debris

But, secretly and importantly,
they are masters of motion

Choreographed, foot-loose, and free.

THINGS I LIKE ABOUT YUMA

★

Like
Sunsets
Occasional rain
Soft Spring breezes
Roadrunners in my yard
Finding lizards in my shower
Toads croaking at the wash basin
Martinez Lake on a hot summer day
Catching a catfish and frying it for dinner
Watching hot air balloons lift off in early morning
Hiking in Palm Canyon and seeing beautiful Bighorn Sheep
Walking in the Annual Veteran's Day Parade dressed as a clown
Tumbleweeds dancing across the empty fields on a cold windy March day
No snow
Dust devils
Cotton fields
Lettuce Fields
Hummingbirds
Marine jets flying
Fruit from my yard

WATER

Haiku

Water rolling down
Feeling the quench of life's juice
Oh, to have a drop

WHISPERING SAGUARO

As new snow gently falls
on a hushed desert night,
Saguaro cactus quietly lift their arms
to catch the soft snowflakes,
and whisper a sigh
as the cold, wet snow lands softly
on each needle,
and the desert is covered
in a white blanket of sparkling wonder,
as a full moon beams down upon them.

YUMA COUNTY FAIR

The lights, the sounds, the magic,
the smell of popcorn, cotton candy, and fried bread.
Those thrilling loopy-de-loop rides,
that illicit high pitched screams, and laughters of joy.
The games of toss and throw and strength,
that challenge even the best athletes.

We wait impatiently for it to begin,
to walk the Midway,
nibbling on a frozen banana,
or a sausage on a stick,
and sipping cold, cold limeade,
with a spray-painted flying disk in our hand.

We visit the small animal barn,
with rabbits, and ducks, and chickens, and guinea pigs,
as the feathery turkeys strut around protecting their turf.
The large animal area houses those stunning steer,
the gentle lambs, playful veal, and comical, snorting pigs,
as nanny goats and billy goats run around
looking for anything to chew on.

The Yuma County Fair comes but once a year,
but the memories of the sideshows, spring breezes,
tastes, sights, and smells,

carry us through the long, hot summer days
when the scorching heat confines us
to indoor air conditioning,
and we sew, quilt, craft, and prepare for next year's fair.